HOW TO WIN THE LOTTERY WITH THE LAW OF ATTRACTION:

FOUR LOTTERY WINNERS SHARE THEIR MANIFESTATION TECHNIQUES

Eddie Coronado

CONTENTS

DEDICATION:

This book is dedicated to the Law of Attraction lottery winners whom I interviewed for this book, and to the legendary metaphysical teacher and writer Stuart Wilde, who helped me understand the true nature of the Universal Law.

The Universal Law does not care whether you have your heart's desire or not. Therefore, you might as well make up your mind to collect.

—Stuart Wilde, *Miracles*

YOU CAN WIN THE LOTTERY WITH THE LAW OF ATTRACTION

I am a Law of Attraction lottery winner and author of the book titled "Manifest Your Millions: A Lottery Winner Shares his Law of Attraction Secrets," which is available on Amazon.com. My book clearly explains what the Law of Attraction is, what it responds to, and how to use it effectively. My testimony is unique because I am an actual lottery winner who has successfully used the Law of Attraction to manifest lottery prizes. Throughout the years I have taught thousands of people how to harness the power of the Universal Law through my written materials, CDs, and during Law of Attraction workshops. One of the most notable facts I have learned about the Universal Law is that this power is available to any person who is willing to learn about its characteristics and then implement a plan of action until the desired manifestation has occurred. *The Universal Law cannot say no to you because its nature is to create circumstances based upon the quality of your thoughts, feelings and beliefs.* It will respond to your prolonged thoughts and feelings by delivering your desires ASAP or by delaying the manifestation until you have clarified your intention, and then cultivated the necessary belief that is needed to translate your desire from the invisible realm of thoughts to the physical world of manifestation. *This power cannot say no to you because it is impartial and has absolutely no opinion about what you should or should not have.* And because its nature is not to refuse your requests, it will give you anything that you can make a part of your beliefs and feelings. As a result, many people throughout the world have used this power to prosper on many levels, to win big lottery prizes, casino jackpots, cars, houses, contests, sweepstakes, money, and other wonderful prizes. And the wonderful truth is that you can use this creative power, too! In fact, it is waiting for you to step up and claim what is yours by divine right.

HOW I BECAME A LAW OF ATTRACTION LOTTERY WINNER

Shortly after learning about the Law of Attraction, I decided to manifest a considerable amount of money to pay off bills and to get out of debt, so I established an intention to attract $50,000.00 through the creative power of the Universal Law. I chose the sum of $50,000.00 because I was a new student of the Law of Attraction at the time, and this particular dollar amount "felt" like something that I could mentally and emotionally accept at the time. My first impulse was to manifest a larger amount of money, but because I was new to these teachings and did not have much experience manifesting

2

money up to that point, I made that particular amount of money my intention. A few months after establishing my intention, I won $50,000.00 in the California Lottery! Since then I have won several smaller prizes and one larger prize through the Law of Attraction. In addition, I have used the Law of Attraction to create a lucrative business, to travel extensively, and to enjoy my life in many wonderful ways through the use of this creative power. As a result of my success and the success of others, I have no doubt that every individual has an inherent creative potential that can be used to attract money, a partner, a new car, a new job, a place to live, or even a lottery prize. The only limits we have are those that we place upon ourselves through a lack of belief. Therefore, the purpose of this book is to help you expand your beliefs to manifest the money that you desire through the creative power of the Universal Law.

WHY YOU SHOULD READ THIS BOOK

Throughout the years I have spoken to a number of people who have used the Law of Attraction to win lottery and contest prizes. I have met these people through friends, at spiritual workshops and via the Internet. One particular lottery winner is named Melissa, who won $1,000,000.00 on the lottery through the Law of Attraction. Another lottery winner is named Jonathan, who won $2,000,000.00 on a lottery ticket after learning about the Law of Attraction and then implementing a plan of action that included the manifestation techniques presented in this book. The purpose of this book is to document the manifestation techniques used by people who have actually won big lottery prizes through the creative power of intention. So, as you read this book please be sure to take notes because some of this information must be understood thoroughly in order to be used effectively. This book contains exactly what is necessary to give you the metaphysical winning edge when playing games of chance.

INTRODUCTION:

E verybody wants to win the lottery! It's one of the most exciting events that can happen in a person's life! Take it from a real winner---there is nothing else quite like it! Along with the excitement of knowing that you have actually beaten the odds, there is the financial benefit of receiving a large amount of cash that can be used to pay off bills, to take a vacation, or to pay off a mortgage. Every day dozens of people win lots of money by playing the various lottery games offered in many countries, states and provinces throughout the world. Some of the most popular scratch off tickets offer top prizes ranging from $500 to over one million dollars. In fact, California offers many games in which the top prize is one million dollars. At the time of this writing there is even a scratch off game that offers a top prize of $5,000.00 per week for 25 years. In New York you can buy a scratch off ticket that offers a top prize of $10,000.00 per week for life, and another exciting game that offers a payout of $1,000,000.00 a year for life! Various states also offer daily Pick 5 games that advertise jackpots starting at $50,000.00 and roll over until a winner has been made. The big money, however, is offered by multi-state drawings such as Mega Millions and

Powerball. In Europe, The National Lottery has made many people very rich, and in Canada the Lotto 6/49 and Lotto Max continue to turn out new millionaires regularly.

A notable fact about the lottery is that every once in a while a lottery player admits to using the Law of Attraction to win a jackpot! Some major newspapers and television networks have even carried stories about people who have used the creative power of intention to manifest their own lottery jackpot. To date, the most famous Law of Attraction lottery story centers around a woman named Cynthia Stafford who used the Law of Attraction to win a Mega Millions jackpot of $112,000,000.00. While appearing on the Ricki Lake Television Show, she revealed to the awestruck audience that she used the Law of Attraction to win her jackpot, and she even explained that she was inspired by the Universe to pick the winning numbers. *It was no surprise when she won because she faithfully used the creative power of her imagination to manifest her desired reality.* On a similar note, the legendary metaphysical teacher named Stuart Wilde told the story about a woman who used the Law of Attraction to win over $2,000,000.00 in her state lottery. And more recently, a Los Angeles man won $5,000,000.00 on a scratch off ticket shortly after clarifying that his intention was to win the lottery. His story was covered in the local print and television news broadcasts shortly after his win.

The Law of Attraction can be used to win all types of lottery prizes, sweepstakes and contests. In fact, Helen Hadsell is probably one of the most famous Law of Attraction contest winners in the world. She has used the creative power of intention to win a car, overseas vacations, a new house, tens of thousands of dollars in cash, and several thousand prizes that include furniture, appliances and household items. As a result, she is known as "The woman who wins every contest prize she desires" by writers, radio and television interviewers around the world. Her manifestation method is similar to the manifestation techniques used by the Law of Attraction lottery winners I have interviewed, which proves that there is a creative power available to anyone who is willing to understand it and use it effectively.

THIS BOOK CONTAINS FOUR PARTS:

PART 1: This section explores the tools that are used for the manifestation techniques in this book. The tools covered are as follows: Affirmations, Creative Visualization, Expectation, Gratitude, and the Practice of Receiving. You should take the time to carefully read this section even if you are familiar with the Law of Attraction and the power of intention. This section contains a number of insights and explanations that may have been missed by other authors and teachers. For example, the Practice of Receiving is a powerful tool that can help you attract a lot of money, yet many Law of Attraction books do not mention this important exercise. In addition, I have included some helpful information about gratitude and affirmations as it relates to manifesting money. Affirmations of words, thoughts, feelings, and actions are also covered. *Finally, the* *most important element of any manifestation technique is creative visualization, which every Law of Attraction lottery winner and contest winner has used to win prizes.*

PART 2: This section includes the manifestation techniques used by the winners who were interviewed for this book. Each winner, including the author, is introduced and his/her manifestation exercise is documented to reflect the exact steps taken to win lottery prizes. No changes have been made in order to preserve the integrity of each winner's method. After each exercise has been explored, various questions and answers are addressed so that the reader may gain additional insights in order to use these manifestation techniques effectively.

PART 3: This is a Question and Answer Section that covers the most important questions about the manifestation techniques in this book. The answers have been provided by the lottery winners who were interviewed. This Question and Answer section will provide clarity and direction for those readers who are committed to using the Law of Attraction to manifest lottery prizes. The questions included in this section cover topics such as: Should I buy lots of tickets? How will I know that my intention will work? How long will it take for me to get results? What part does luck play in manifesting lottery prizes? In addition, a host of other important questions are discussed.

PART 4: This section contains helpful tips and suggestions that will explain how to implement the following manifestation techniques and how to make the most of them. It also contains information regarding the common denominators of the winners' daily action plan in order to provide a clear understanding of the mental and emotional habits that are necessary for manifesting lottery prizes through the Law of Attraction.

PART 1: THE TOOLS

In order to manifest the desires of your heart through the creative power of intention you must add the necessary ingredient of ACTION to the Law of Attr-ACTION. Without daily, consistent action on your part, you will hinder the manifestation of your desires through this immensely creative power. As a result, the following metaphysical tools and techniques will help you manifest what you desire through the Law of Attraction. This list is presented in alphabetical order, and each tool is equally important when used purposefully and consistently.

AFFIRMATIONS: The lottery winners whose manifestation techniques are included in this book have used spoken affirmations to assist in the creation of their desired reality. They understood the creative power of words and the role they play in influencing day to day events. As a result, these winners repeated affirmative statements throughout the day and were mindful of all the words they spoke throughout the day. Melissa, whose manifestation technique is the first covered in this book, made the following statement in an e-mail message from her home in New York City: "I never joked about money and never said anything negative about it. If I didn't have something positive to say about money, I didn't say anything at all. This way there was nothing to cancel my positive affirmations and the feelings of wealth that I was creating all day long." Jonathan, the second winner interviewed for this book, made the following statement in an e-mail message prior to our interview: "I spoke positive words and used creative visualization to manifest my lottery prize. I became so positive and expectant that I wasn't surprised when I won. Words are creative because they have the power to make you feel expectant." Jonathan's message reminded me of the early 2014 news reports of a man from the UK who won a huge National Lottery jackpot of nearly 108,000,000 British Pounds, which is roughly equivalent to $180,000,000.00. His story was reported around the world, and reporters particularly took note of the fact that the day before his big win, he confidently told many of his close friends and family members, "This time tomorrow I'll be a millionaire!" The EuroMillions winner went on to say that he always thought he would win big and that he "had a good feeling all week." In light of this information, it should be noted that all words are creative, including words spoken in casual conversation and words repeated as affirmations. A person who is serious about manifesting wealth through the Law of Attraction must monitor everything that he or she says. Every word spoken must be considered creative, and will contribute to the overall mental atmosphere of the person making the statements. *A person cannot be negative one minute and still expect the Universal Law to deliver his/her desires unaffected.* As a result, you must provide a positive, expectant mindset in order to make this power work effectively.

In addition, the most effective affirmations should reflect the following qualities:

- Spoken affirmations should be short and to the point because they lose their effectiveness if they are too wordy. *The mental energy required to remember a long affirmation is better spent in feeling the reality of a short, powerful affirmation.*

- Spoken affirmations should be positive, uplifting, and they should make you feel expectant when repeating them.

- Spoken affirmations should be repeated throughout the day. A statement only spoken once during the day is not an affirmation.

- All the words you speak are affirmations to the Universal Law of what you are and what you want to have more of. Therefore, you should monitor all the words you speak because there is creative power in every word you utter.

CREATIVE VISUALIZATION: Each of the winners in this book has used the creative power of imagination to win a lottery prize. Daily, each person spent time visualizing his or her desire as a wish fulfilled. Jonathan excelled in the use of creative visualization because he felt comfortable using his imagination to experience his desires as completed facts. During a telephone call one evening, he explained:

"I did not feel enthusiastic about using affirmations alone, so I added positive dialogue to my creative visualization exercises, which helped me feel expectant and made the exercises a lot more fun." Jonathan's creative visualization exercise will provide more insight into his particular manifestation technique. The two ladies who were interviewed, however, enjoyed using spoken affirmations but they experienced some resistance when trying to visualize their desires as completed facts. They later learned to overcome these challenges by incorporating affirmative words into their creative visualization exercises.

It should be noted that men and women are emotionally "wired" differently, so they often have much different experiences with spoken affirmations and creative visualization exercises. Men are more inclined to get excited about what they can see or visualize, such as a home run, a sports car, or an attractive person. As a result, men have a head start in the area of creative visualization but sometimes lack the motivation to repeat affirmations regularly. Women, on the other hand, are emotionally wired in a way that is highly responsive to words, the lyrics to a song, or the words written on a greeting card. As a result, women have a head start in the area of spoken affirmations and tend to excel in this area. Of course, there are some men and women who equally enjoy using spoken affirmations and creative visualization exercises. This idea has been presented in order to make the reader more aware of the dynamics of the human personality as it relates to using the Law of Attraction effectively. The following manifestation techniques will address how each winner benefitted through the use of spoken affirmations and creative visualization in spite of their individual challenges.

EXPECTATION: Expectation is one of the most powerful tools you will use as a co-creator with the Universal Law. Every Law of Attraction lottery winner has successfully used the power of expectation to manifest a jackpot. *It is very important to understand that the Universal Law is set in motion through the power of feelings, and it will faithfully respond to all expectant feelings whether they are positive or negative.* Expectation is a feeling that is based in the certainty that an event will take place. In this book you will be exposed to manifestation techniques that will help you increase your expectation of manifesting money. Similar to the way an athlete expects to build muscles with each successive workout, you can expect to manifest your desires as you perform the mental and emotional exercises described in this book. We must incorporate action into our daily schedule otherwise we cannot expect the Law of Attraction to deliver our desires. This book will help you understand what you can do each day to manifest your desires through this creative power.

GRATITUDE: Gratitude is a powerful metaphysical tool that you can use to align yourself with financial abundance and prosperity. The grateful feelings that you express will attract more good things to be grateful for because all persistent feelings will attract matching circumstances. This is why people who are thankful attract more things to be thankful for while those who complain always attract more events and circumstances to complain about. The legendary inventor and mechanical engineer Nikola Tesla wrote, "If you want to find the secrets of the universe, think in terms of energy, frequency and vibration." As we express feelings of gratitude on a regular basis, our energy, frequency and vibration will attract events and circumstances to match these predominant feelings. So, as you practice the following manifestation techniques, be sure to fill your thoughts with gratitude for all that you have and for all that comes your way, even if what you currently have is very little. For starters, as you commit to the following manifestation techniques you should be thankful for the money that you have to play your favorite lottery games. You should also be thankful for any lottery prizes that you collect along the way to manifesting your desired jackpot. Some people enjoy speaking words of gratitude for all the good things that come to them while others use a gratitude journal to write about everything they are thankful for. The method used is not as important as your daily commitment to the act of gratitude. The popular statement "whatever you THANK about, you bring about" is not only a catchy phrase but a statement of great metaphysical importance.

THE PRACTICE OF RECEIVING: The Practice of Receiving is one of the most powerful Law of Attraction exercises that a person can use to attract more money. For starters, when you are willing to receive all that comes your way you are affirming to the Universal Law that you are open and willing to receive more good things. By refusing what is offered to you, you are affirming to the same creative power that you are not willing to receive whatever comes your way. Do not take the practice of receiving lightly. Learn to say yes when a co-worker offers to pay for your lunch or when someone offers you a cup of coffee, and make sure you always pick up the pennies you find on the sidewalk. This exercise is not about collecting coffee and pennies. It's a powerful metaphysical exercise that will open your mind to the flow of abundance as you begin to accept more. *In addition, if you affirm and visualize for prosperity yet you deny the flow of abundance in your life, you have canceled your prosperity intention. Your thoughts, feelings, words and actions are all affirmations to the Universal Law of who you are, so be sure to affirm abundance and prosperity in all that you do.* The author of this book has used the Practice of Receiving to align himself to prosperity and abundance. The manifestation techniques in this book will further explain how to use this powerful tool to prosper.

PART 2: THE MANIFESTATION TECHNIQUES

To play the game of life successfully, we must become aware of our every mental activity, for this activity, in the form of inner conversations, is the cause of the outer phenomena of our life.
—Neville Goddard

Law of Attraction Lottery Winner #1: Melissa

I was introduced to Melissa during a Sunday service at Unity Church in Los Angeles. Although Melissa has since gotten married and moved to New York City we remain in regular contact by telephone and through e-mail. Throughout the years Melissa has won a number of $500 prizes on scratch off tickets and a Powerball prize of $1,000,000.00 by matching five numbers on a single ticket. After watching the movie THE SECRET and learning about the creative power of thoughts, Melissa created an intention to win a "big lottery prize" through the Universal Law. While she did not specify exactly how much money she intended to win, she used the creative power of visualization to imagine winning a lottery prize large enough to pay off her bills, buy a new car, and to take a vacation to Sydney, Australia. As a result, she always set the tone of her morning through the use of spoken affirmations, which she enjoyed repeating throughout the day. The night I called for the telephone interview she explained that spoken affirmations always made her feel good, so she made them a part of her daily Law of Attraction schedule. Her favorite affirmation for financial abundance is: *"Miracles never cease! My life is overflowing with abundance, prosperity, and lots of money."* Although she experimented with a number of affirmations that she found in books, she claimed that she felt more positive and expectant using this particular affirmation because she wrote it, so its words had subjective meaning for her. She asked me to let my readers know that she always used affirmations that made her feel positive and expectant when repeating them. She also kept a small notebook filled with her favorite affirmations for prosperity and success.

Ever since Melissa was a teenager she has been well aware of the power of intention and in her ability to prosper through the creative use of thoughts and feelings. As a young lady she was introduced to the prosperity teachings of Catherine Ponder, whom she heard speak a number of times during Unity Church services and at prosperity workshops in Southern California. Catherine Ponder's book titled THE DYNAMIC LAWS OF PROSPERITY is Melissa's all-time favorite book on the subject, but she also claims to have been influenced by the legendary teachings of Neville Goddard, whose basic message is that "imagining creates reality." For over forty years Neville Goddard taught millions of people throughout the world that the human imagination is the creative power of God in action, and that anyone can influence events in the physical world through the controlled and persistent use of imagination. Although Neville has been deceased for a number of years, his books and teachings are so well known throughout the world that he was quoted in the popular Law of Attraction book titled THE SECRET. Melissa's favorite book by Neville Goddard is THE LAW AND THE PROMISE because it is very practical, easy to read, and has lots of success stories. She claimed that Neville Goddard's teachings encouraged her to use the power of creative visualization to manifest the financial abundance she desired. To date, she has manifested a lucrative career, a new home in Brooklyn, profitable rental property, and lottery prizes through the creative power of her thoughts and feelings.

Melissa's Manifestation Technique:

Several times a day Melissa would imagine holding a large, symbolic lottery check with her name printed on it. She would imagine standing at lottery headquarters, surrounded by excited onlookers who congratulate her on winning a big prize. As she felt the reality of being a lottery winner, she would imagine hearing the words "Congratulations on winning the lottery!" and then she would mentally respond with statements such as "Thank You!" and "I always knew I would win the lottery!" She performed this mental exercise over and over again until the expectation and excitement of a lottery win was a natural part of her beliefs and feelings.

Melissa would then imagine arriving at the bank to deposit her lottery check. She would mentally see the bank teller congratulating her on winning a jackpot, and she would excitedly respond by saying, "Thank You! I love the feeling of being a lottery winner! I always knew I would win." She would visualize the bank teller counting out her cash withdrawal of several thousand dollars, handing it to her, and then wishing her a wonderful vacation in Australia. This exercise made her feel very positive and expectant.

Since shopping always made Melissa feel happy, she would then visualize how having lots of shopping money would make her feel. She would feelingly experience the reality of having lots of money by imagining that her wallet was filled with cash. As she performed this exercise she would mentally ask herself the question: How does having lots of spending money make me feel? How would I feel if I could go to a store and buy anything I wanted? She would then imagine shopping at the Macy's department store in Manhattan. While in her imaginary store she would create scenes in which she would say to the sales clerk, "I will take this purse. I am paying cash." She always felt good while doing this manifestation exercise and these prosperous feelings encouraged her to visualize more often.

Melissa performed this mental exercise at least three times a day with presence of mind, feeling and clarity. When she had extra time on her hands, she did it more than three times a day because the prosperous feelings she experienced felt very good and became addictive. She did this exercise morning, noon and just before bed. She often fell asleep imagining herself holding a large, symbolic lottery check while feeling the excitement of a big lottery win. She soon realized that large lottery checks were made of a thick cardboard-like paper, so she incorporated this fact into her exercises by imagining the weight of this oversized check, thereby adding another dimension of reality to this exercise.

During a phone call one evening Melissa explained that nothing out of the ordinary happened at first, but she persisted with her manifestation exercise and practiced gratitude with every win, even if she only won a few dollars or a free ticket. As she persisted with this daily ritual, she began to feel increasingly expectant about receiving a lot of money, and soon she won a prize of $1,000,000.00 on a quick pick she bought one morning on the way to work. Melissa excitedly told me, "Every Sunday morning I check my tickets over a cup of coffee. Well, I nearly spit up my coffee when I realized that I had won! The following morning I was at the lottery office to cash in my ticket. The lottery official congratulated me, and it was like Deja vu when I said: 'Thank you! I always knew I would win!'"

Melissa went on to explain that she had experimented with a number of creative visualization exercises, but she felt most comfortable using the exercise in which she held the large lottery check. She told me that this scenario felt "natural" to her because she enjoyed seeing winners holding oversized checks at the televised press conferences. She also explained that her creative visualization exercise did not take on life until she added dialogue to it. She said that it was easier to feel the reality of this exercise when she imagined hearing statements such as: "Congratulations on winning the lottery!" and "I always knew I would win!" I explained to her that since some people are more responsive to spoken words, dialogue can be added to these manifestation exercises for better results. As a result of the imagined dialogue in her manifestation exercises, she felt enthusiastic about doing them regularly because the words added a dimension of reality that increased her expectation. Before our telephone call was over, I asked Melissa if she wanted to share any more information about her manifestation technique, and she immediately replied, "Tell your readers that it's very important to persist in feeling the reality of having lots of money than by figuring out how it will happen. Do the inner work, and then leave the details to the Universe. Visualize daily and always be positive and expectant, and you are guaranteed to attract money."

An important note about expectation is that it can be generated through the use of creative visualization exercises. For example, as we affirm, visualize, and feel the reality of what we desire, we begin to create feelings of expectation within us. *The more we use these exercises, the greater is our expectation.* During the call, Melissa explained that she did not feel expectant at first, but her expectation increased as she persisted with her manifestation exercises. Creative visualization helps us become comfortable with what we want on an emotional level, and the more we imagine doing and having the things we desire, the more comfortable we become with these things.

Law of Attraction Lottery Winner #2: Jonathan

I met Jonathan during a meditation workshop at a metaphysical book store in Los Angeles, California. He was happy to share his experiences with the Law of Attraction because he had recently manifested some wonderful things through the creative power of his thoughts, including a big lottery prize. I told him that I had also used the Law of Attraction to win lottery prizes, and a friendship instantly blossomed. Although he had a busy schedule, he made time to meet me for lunch one afternoon at Canter's, a popular Los Angeles deli. I told Jonathan that I was writing a book with the purpose of sharing the manifestation techniques of Law of Attraction lottery winners, and he was more than happy to share his insights and manifestation techniques.

Although Jonathan first learned about the Law of Attraction when he was twenty, he did not start using it intentionally until he was in his mid-thirties. By that time, he was ready for a major change in life and was hopeful that he could turn his life around by thinking more positive thoughts and by using the power of creative visualization. Throughout his twenties he struggled with money issues and held down an office job that kept him just above the poverty level. With the money earned at work he was able to pay for rent and groceries, but he seemed to consistently lack the necessary funds to enjoy life on a larger scale by eating at fine restaurants more often, buying the clothes he wanted, and driving the car of his dreams. His dream of financial freedom eluded him until he committed to harnessing the creative power of his thoughts, words and feelings. When I met Jonathan he was attending the Church of Religious Science, which exposed him to the idea that all thoughts, words and feelings are creative. The teachings of Dr. Ernest Holmes, who founded the church, are taught within this spiritual community and throughout the world. Dr. Holmes was a great spiritual teacher and visionary whose fundamental message is that we have the power to change our lives by changing our thoughts. With this knowledge in mind, Jonathan began paying close attention to all his words, thoughts and feelings with the understanding that he had the power to create a more positive life based upon the quality of his mental state. Little by little, as Jonathan cleared up his mental act and visualized daily, he began seeing positive changes in his personal and financial life. As a result of his commitment to inner growth, he entered a wonderful relationship with a lady he met at church, he got a better paying job, and he soon won $2,000,000.00 on a lottery ticket that he bought one evening on the way home from work. He usually bought Mega Millions tickets but decided to buy a scratch off ticket when he saw that the grand prize was $2,000,000.00. It was on this ticket that he won his big prize. He said that he didn't scratch his ticket that evening because he was in a hurry to pick up his girlfriend for dinner, but he made a mental note to scratch it the following morning before leaving to work. That particular morning was, according to his words, "the most exciting morning of my life so far! I screamed so loud that I scared my dog!"

Jonathan eventually learned to use the creative power of words to influence his reality. "My life was once falling apart in many different areas," Jonathan confessed as lunch was being served, "and it was a result of the negative words I was using to describe my life." He went on to say that he had once been a negative thinker who used the power of his words carelessly. He confessed, "I would always joke about money, and I kept myself in lack and limitation through my negative words. When I stopped joking about my money situation and learned to speak positively about money, my life began to change for the better. It started slowly at first, then it started influencing every area of my life in a positive way." Jonathan then explained how he used the creative power of his spoken word to attract prosperity and abundance. Each time he bought a lottery ticket he would say to the clerk: "Give me the big winning ticket!" In fact, he never bought a lottery ticket unless he made this particular statement. His expectant demeanor was so familiar with store clerks that they often smiled and said to him, "You're here for the big winning ticket!"

Jonathan's Manifestation Technique:

Three times a day Jonathan would imagine what it would feel like to win the lottery. He would visualize himself saying to the store cashier, "I'll take the big winning ticket," and then he would imagine the excitement of realizing that it was a winner. Using focused attention and as much excitement as he could mentally and emotionally create, he would imagine telling his best friend that he had won the lottery. He persisted in feeling the excitement that he would experience upon realizing that he was a lottery winner. As he visualized he would ask himself, "How would I feel to win the lottery?" And then he would imagine those feelings with as much vividness and emotional intensity as he could imagine. He would then imagine calling his girlfriend to tell her that he had won a jackpot. He would experience the same excitement that he would feel if he had actually won, and then he would imagine her congratulating him. This exercise felt so good that he would do it over and over as he became totally immersed in the feeling of being a lottery winner. As far as his feelings were concerned, there was no question that he was a lottery winner.

In order to prolong his positive and expectant feelings, Jonathan would then imagine owning and driving the car of his dreams, a Corvette. He would imagine visiting the Chevrolet dealership and telling the salesperson that he was there to buy his dream car. In his imagination he would hear the salesperson ask if financing was needed, and Jonathan would respond, "I can pay cash." He would imagine completing the purchase, and then he felt the reality of driving his new car off the lot. Using as much focused attention and emotion as he could create within his imagination, he would experience the reality of driving home his dream car knowing that the purchase was possible because of his lottery win. He would always end his exercise by imagining that his friends were congratulating him on his good fortune. He would mentally hear his girlfriend and best friend tell him "Congratulations on winning the lottery!" and "You're the luckiest guy I know!"

As we continued eating I took the opportunity to delve deeper into Jonathan's creative visualization exercise in order to gain more clarity about his manifestation technique. I was curious to know what the most important aspect of his exercise was, but I was not kept waiting for an answer. Jonathan immediately responded, "During my exercises, I spent quality time imagining what I would do with my prize money. I mentally saw myself eating at nice restaurants, going on vacations, and having lots of money in my bank account and my wallet. It was important for me to play an active role in these mental scenes." Jonathan explained that his creative visualization exercises included all the words he would say, the things he would do, and the words and actions of the other people in his imaginary scenes. Jonathan's approach is similar to that of another lottery winner from Michigan, who won $66,000,000.00 on the Mega Millions game in 2014. During the official press conference at lottery headquarters, the 24 year old Michigan winner told reporters, "I always dreamed about winning *and what I would do with the money."*

Since the question of "How long will it take?" often comes up during Law of Attraction workshops, I decided to ask Jonathan how long it took to manifest his lottery win. He answered by saying that winning his prize took about six months of committed spiritual work that included creative visualization exercises and affirmations. His favorite affirmation was: *"I love the thought of being a lottery winner. I am the luckiest guy I know, and I always attract lots of money and financial abundance."* Jonathan told me that his manifestation took time because he had to work past the negativity and doubt that was in his mind, but as he committed to this spiritual work he gradually transformed his limiting beliefs and became comfortable with having lots of money. "Six months of commitment," said Jonathan, "is what it usually takes me to make a major manifestation because that's how long it takes to establish my intention and then visualize my desire into manifestation."

I then asked Jonathan if he thought that repeating the same exercise day after day was boring. He responded by saying that he would often spice up his manifestation exercise by imagining that he was watching the lottery drawing on TV. "As I did this," Jonathan explained, "I would imagine how I would feel to match all the numbers on my ticket. I would also imagine that my picture was on the lottery website showing me as a winner. These little variations helped me break the routine of doing the same exercise every day."

Before we finished our meals and left the restaurant I asked Jonathan if he wanted to share any other information about manifesting a lottery prize or a large amount of money through the Law of Attraction. Without missing a beat, he said, "Making the Law of Attraction work is not a matter of being worthy or special. Anyone can use this power to manifest money or anything they want. It's all a matter of doing your part by visualizing daily and acting 'as if' without constantly looking over your shoulder for quick results. The Law of Attraction works if you work it correctly."

Law of Attraction Lottery Winner #3: Jennifer

I met Jennifer through an online Law of Attraction forum. She lives and works in San Francisco, California, and has been studying the Law of Attraction since she was first introduced to these spiritual truths by a coworker. She and I exchanged messages back and forth for a month before we actually chatted on the phone. During our telephone conversation we realized that we both enjoyed traveling and watching classic movies such as REAR WINDOW and VERTIGO, the latter of which was filmed in her hometown of San Francisco. Jennifer is a nurse, mother of two girls, and a lottery winner who used the Law of Attraction to win a Fantasy Five prize of over $200,000.00. During our telephone conversation I mentioned that I would be in San Francisco for the approaching Memorial Day weekend, and we agreed to meet over breakfast to share our spiritual insights. I was more than happy to meet her and learn how she manifested a lottery prize with the Law of Attraction.

On the morning of our interview, I left my motel room on Market Street and walked to the nearby Café Flore to meet Jennifer for breakfast. Located at the intersection of Market, Noe and 16th Streets, it's the perfect place to see the historic streetcars that run up and down Market Street. Upon entering the restaurant, Jennifer and I instantly recognized each other among the waiting crowd because we had exchanged photos via e-mail. After a few moments, we were seated in the patio and ordered breakfast as locals walked by in the crisp morning air.

Unlike the other winners who primarily used creative visualization to manifest lottery jackpots, Jennifer relied on the power of her spoken word to stir up the positive expectancy that was necessary to manifest her lottery prize. Her manifestation technique consisted of three important elements: spoken gratitude, spoken affirmations, and the use of creative visualization. As our breakfast was being served, Jennifer said that affirmations made her feel more positive and expectant than creative visualization, so she focused on what made her feel good by incorporating affirmations into her manifestation exercises. She explained, "It was challenging for me to create mental scenes and to visualize having lots of money, but my spoken affirmations have always made me feel powerful and expectant, so I went that route." As a result, she wrote her own affirmations that helped her feel positive and expectant. Some of her favorite affirmations are as follows:

My mind is a center of divine operation and I now receive all the money and prosperity that I desire through my spoken word. All doors of abundance swing open for me right now!

My spoken word now releases all the financial abundance that is mine by divine right! Unexpected doors open and unexpected channels now release all the money and opportunities that I need.

All avenues of abundant supply are open for me right now. I now receive all the financial abundance that is mine by divine right.

All the money I desire now comes to me under grace in perfect ways!

Jennifer clearly understood that the creative power of words is found in the way they make a person feel. "If an affirmation did not feel right for me," Jennifer said, "I would not use it again. I would rewrite it or use an affirmation that made me feel positive." As I interviewed Jennifer I realized that she understood just how creative words are. During breakfast she made a statement that has been in my thoughts ever since. Her memorable statement was, *"When you realize how powerful your words are, you guard every word that comes out of your mouth."* I had to agree with her statement because I believe in the creative power of words and in their ability to create matching circumstances based upon their nature. Words spoken today might not manifest as circumstances this week, but sometime down the road all the words we speak will meet us with the same creative intensity with which they were spoken. In early 2014 I attended a Wednesday evening service at the Agape International Spiritual

Center in Culver City, California. Dr. Michael Beckwith, who was featured in the movie THE SECRET, delivered a powerful message that night titled: "Your Words: Prophetic or Pathetic?" During his insightful message he talked about the creative power of words and their ability to create matching circumstances. He said that our words are prophetic and must be carefully monitored because of their creative nature. During the interview with Jennifer that morning I realized that she was well aware of the creative power of the spoken word.

Jennifer's Manifestation Technique:

Jennifer's Manifestation Exercise contains three important elements: spoken gratitude, spoken affirmations and creative visualization.

At least three times a day Jennifer would walk around her apartment and give thanks for everything she owned, including her television, the food in her cabinets and even for her comfortable bed. She would also give thanks for the money in her purse and for her job. She would make statements such as, "I am thankful for my job, my apartment, and for all my friends. I am thankful for my children and my boyfriend." As she entered into the spirit of gratitude, she would think about more things to be thankful for, and she would even give thanks for the simple blessings she experiences daily, such as fresh air, her reliable car, and for the coffee that she enjoys each morning. Jennifer believes that a person cannot experience increased prosperity until she can be thankful for what she currently has. She believes that as we express gratitude on a daily basis, we open channels of increased abundance in all areas of life. She said that one sure way to increase finances is to feel thankful for the money that you currently have, even if it is a small amount.

Once Jennifer finished speaking words of gratitude for all her possessions, she would begin speaking the affirmations that she wrote. She would repeat her affirmations until she felt the truth of her words. Her favorite affirmation to begin with was: "My spoken word now releases all the abundance that is mine by divine right! Unexpected doors open and unexpected channels now release all the money and opportunities that I need." As she repeated this affirmation with feeling, she would imagine that her purse was filled with money. She would also imagine that her bank statement reflected a large balance. As she continued to affirm words of abundance, she would feel the reality of owning and driving a new car, shopping for clothes whenever she wanted, and having enough money to save each month. Jennifer's spoken affirmations always made her feel positive and expectant, so she used spoken affirmations as she visualized winning a big lottery prize. While speaking affirmations she would imagine the excitement that she would feel as a lottery winner. She would imagine buying a ticket, checking her numbers after the drawing, and then she would feel the increasing excitement of realizing that she held a winning ticket. She performed this exercise over and over until she felt like she was a lottery winner. Because spoken words made her feel positive and expectant, she would vividly imagine saying to her mother, "I won a big lottery prize! I finally won a jackpot!" And then she would imagine her mother congratulating her on the big win. At the end of the day, she would perform this exercise again just before bed, and then she would fall asleep in the excitement of being a winner. Performing this exercise before sleep would often result in vivid dreams about winning the lottery and having lots of money. Jennifer would wake *up after each of these dreams feeling excited and expectant about her impending manifestation.*

As we sipped coffee I asked Jennifer what she experienced the day of her lottery win. She replied by saying, "The day I won my lottery prize was no different than any other day. I went to work as usual, then picked up dinner and lottery tickets before going home that evening. The store clerk told me that the Fantasy Five jackpot was big that night because it had rolled over, so I decided to buy two tickets." Jennifer was very excited a few days later when she checked her numbers on the lottery website to discover that she had won a big prize. Shortly after receiving her lottery payment, she bought a new Volkswagen and then went shopping for new clothes just as she imagined.

Jennifer is a unique student of the Law of Attraction because she uses a manifestation journal to record her daily progress. Using a large spiral-bound notebook, she writes down new affirmations, makes lists of various things to be thankful for, and she tracks her spiritual progress as she manifests the life of her dreams. As she uses her manifestation journal daily, she remains focused on her goals and records all the good things that happen as a result of her changing consciousness. If she receives a gift, or finds money, or receives a discount at a store, she records it in her manifestation journal so that she can focus on all the good things that happen to her. She claims that the daily use of her journal has helped her become more aware of the increasing abundance that is a result of her daily spiritual work. "My manifestation journal," Jennifer said as we left the restaurant, "has helped me understand that I truly have the power to manifest my dreams through the power of my words, thoughts and feelings."

Jennifer still uses her manifestation journal and continues to use gratitude, affirmations and creative visualization on a daily basis. These days she is enjoying increasing prosperity and abundance in all areas of her life. Although she is very happy with her first major manifestation, her intention is to win at least a million dollars next time. In addition, she is currently working on creating a manifestation journal for students of the Law of Attraction.

Law of Attraction Lottery Winner #4: The author, Eddie Coronado

I won my first lottery prize of $50,000.00 about six months after learning about the Law of Attraction and committing to a daily action plan that included study, spoken affirmations, creative visualization exercises and the practice of receiving. When I first learned about the Law of Attraction there were relatively few books and tapes that clearly explained this creative power and its use. There were some books that defined the Law of Attraction, but fewer that offered step-by-step instructions explaining how this power can be used on a daily basis. As a result of my studies, I learned that the Universal Law cannot work effectively through a person who engages in negative habits such as complaining, bitterness, anger, jealousy, judgment, and strife. *Some people experience delays while attempting to use the Law of Attraction because they fail to understand that the Universal Law cannot manifest FOR us until it can manifest THROUGH us.* These people affirm for prosperity and abundance, they visualize daily, but they fall short of aligning to the nature of the Universal Law because they hold on to negative thoughts and feelings about situations, people, and themselves. The person who wants to manifest money through the Law of Attraction must closely monitor all thoughts in order to use this power effectively. On a personal level, this meant that I had to eliminate all negative thoughts and feelings about situations and people. I also stopped gossiping and complaining because these are negative habits that have the tendency to place a person out of alignment with the Universal Law, which is characterized by peace, balance and harmony. In an effort to be more positive, I learned to spend more time entertaining uplifting thoughts instead of focusing my energy on negativity and inharmonious thoughts and feelings. As I learned to monitor all my thoughts and feelings more closely, my life took on a positive charge. Money came to me much easier, I got raises at work, people gave me gifts, I took wonderful trips more often, and I won some wonderful lottery prizes. These fortunate events were proof that I had finally learned to harness the power of the Universal Law through positive living and thinking.

I also learned that I would have better results with the Law of Attraction if I allowed this creative power to manifest my desire for more money through any channel of expression. In other words, I did not limit the Universal Law by expecting it to manifest my desire for lots of money through the lottery. *I wanted to win a big lottery prize, and I regularly purchased tickets, but I realized that a lottery win was among the many channels through which my financial abundance could materialize. As a result, I was open to receiving money from any channel that the Universal Law allowed. I feel that this is an important point to mention because the infinite, creative power of the Universal Law is unlimited and has the power to manifest our desires from any number of channels.* It can manifest a cure for cancer just as easily as it can manifest ten million dollars for the person who uses this power correctly and consistently. Because I was open to receiving money from any number of channels, lots of money came into my life through expected and unexpected channels.

An important metaphysical habit that I adopted at this time was the practice of receiving. I learned about this powerful practice in a lecture by a popular spiritual teacher named Stuart Wilde. He stressed the importance of being a good receiver as a way to connect to the ever expanding flow of abundance in the universe. As a result, I learned to say yes to whatever came my way in terms of money, gifts, meals, or anything that was offered to me, even if it was something small and insignificant, such as a cup of coffee. My acceptance of whatever came my way was a repeated affirmation to the Universal Law that I was a good receiver who was open to receiving prosperity. As a result, I picked up all the pennies that I found on the sidewalk as affirmations that I was open to receiving financial prosperity and abundance from the Universal Law. At first, I felt a bit uncomfortable saying yes to everything that people offered me, but I became more comfortable as I practiced receiving on a daily basis. *The practice of receiving helped me realize that my positive actions were attracting greater opportunities, and it helped me learn a very important lesson, which is that affirmations of action are just as important as affirmations of thought and word.*

If I affirmed that I was rich and prosperous, for example, but I passed up a free meal or a gift, I was making a very strong statement to the Universal Law about my willingness to receive. Therefore it is very important to say yes to whatever comes your way even if you end up giving it away. As you learn to become a better receiver, the Universe will send you bigger and better things to receive. The Universal Law is able and willing to manifest all the money we desire, but we must align to this power in thought, word and action in a way that reflects the perfect union of our thoughts and actions. As I got into the spirit of accepting everything that came my way, I began to receive money in many wonderful ways: I was given money, found money, got discounts at restaurants, won numerous casino jackpots and contests, and I eventually won lots of money through the lottery. As I reflect on my spiritual development, I can honestly say that the practice of receiving was one of the most powerful tools that I used on a daily basis because it helped me feel expectant and excited about manifesting more wonderful things, especially money. As I generated strong feelings of expectation through the practice of receiving, the money I desired came to me easily and effortlessly in the form of lottery prizes and through other channels of expression. *A person who wants to manifest money through the Law of Attraction must become a good receiver.*

Another powerful tool that I learned to enjoy and appreciate is creative visualization. For at least a century insightful teachers, spiritual writers and enlightened masters have taught about the immense power of creative visualization. In more recent times, new age writers, motivational speakers, workshop facilitators and athletes have demonstrated the power of creative visualization in goal setting and accomplishment. In a nutshell, creative visualization is a spiritual exercise that anyone can use to change outer circumstances by changing thoughts, feelings and expectations. As we take time to visualize our desires, we accomplish a number of goals on a spiritual level:

- Creative visualization helps us clarify what is important to us.

- Creative visualization helps us create a mental blueprint of our desires.

- Creative visualization helps us become comfortable with what we desire. *If we do not feel comfortable with what we desire, we will find that its manifestation is impossible.* The more comfortable we are with having lots of money, the easier it will manifest through the Law of Attraction.

Eddie's Manifestation Technique:

Three times a day for fifteen minutes each session, I would sit somewhere comfortable and imagine that I was rich. I would experience the reality of owning a Gucci wallet filled with $100 bills. I also imagined having lots of cash in my pockets and in my bank account, and I would imagine having several bundles of one hundred dollar bills in my hands. As I imagined having lots of money, I felt the reality of spending and saving as much money as I desired. In my mind, I saw myself at the mall buying clothes, shoes, and cologne. I also imagined eating at expensive restaurants with friends. As I performed this exercise, I affirmed: "I *have all the money and financial prosperity that I need to live a rich and abundant lifestyle. I always have lots of money to spend and save." As I mentally repeated these words, I felt the truth of these statements. I always began my creative visualization exercise this way in order to establish a strong feeling of prosperity and abundance. I performed this exercise even if feeling rich and prosperous was challenging. Eventually, it became easy to feel rich and prosperous as I persisted with this manifestation exercise.*

Part two of this exercise involved me visualizing that I was a lottery winner. I would imagine checking my lottery ticket, and then I would feel increasing excitement as I realized that my ticket matched all the winning numbers drawn. I felt exactly what I would feel had I matched all the numbers drawn. I imagined telling friends and family members that I was a lottery winner, and I vividly imagined how it would feel to be at the lottery office to sign the paperwork required to collect my winnings. I mentally saw the clerk at the lottery office congratulating me on my win. The most important aspect of this exercise is that I tried to feel exactly how I would feel as a winner. Throughout the exercise I would occasionally ask myself, 'How would I feel if I won the lottery?' and then I would use my imagination to feel the excitement of being a winner. I would do this over and over again with feeling and presence of mind until I felt the reality of winning the lottery.

As mentioned, it took approximately six months of committed spiritual work to manifest a lottery prize of $50,000.00. As I continued to use the Law of Attraction on a daily basis I won another prize of $193,600.00. During this time I was very committed to learning as much as I could about the Law of Attraction while doing the daily exercises that would help me manifest my desires. An important fact I learned about the Law of Attraction is that it is not a stagnant power, but a force that is set in motion through committed, daily action. This is where many people get stuck because they read lots of books about the Law of Attraction, but they fail to use this power effectively through a lack of daily commitment. This power is more than willing to manifest the desires of your heart, but you must learn to work with it through your thoughts, feelings and actions on a consistent basis.

PART 3: QUESTION & ANSWER SECTION

QUESTION: Should I buy lots of lottery tickets?

A NSWER: Absolutely not. You should buy a few tickets and stick to a budget. The creative power within you does not require lots of tickets to work. *In fact, by purchasing a lot of tickets you actually affirm that you are unsure about winning.* Purchasing a few tickets allows you to concentrate your intentional power, and you will have better results this way. Throughout the years many people have won big lottery jackpots, sweepstakes, contests, and other wonderful prizes by purchasing one or two tickets. In May 2013 a lady in Florida won a jackpot of nearly 600 million dollars with one single ticket, and in California a man who believed in the creative power of intention won a lottery jackpot with one single scratch off ticket, so it is not necessary to buy lots of tickets to win. The important fact is to create a consciousness of abundance in your thoughts and feelings so that you will manifest the money you desire.

QUESTION: Will my feelings of desperation help me win faster?

ANSWER: Feelings of desperation have their roots in unbelief and fear. Your feelings of desperation are very strong affirmations to the Universal Law that you do not believe that you can or will manifest money. *As long as you feel desperate, you will manifest more things to feel desperate about.* Hoping to win a big lottery prize while feeling desperate will result in failure. You can transform your feelings of desperation into feelings of expectation by doing the exercises in this book mindfully and persistently. As you visualize and imagine a prosperous reality, your feelings and expectations will gradually change to reflect an expanded awareness and belief that prosperity and abundance are normal and natural for you. *As you change your feelings from financial limitation to prosperity and abundance, your outer experience will change to reflect your new beliefs.*

QUESTION: How can I know that my intention will manifest?

ANSWER: If your creative visualization exercises bring up feelings of expectation and excitement, then you can be sure that your intention contains the inherent power to manifest the things you desire. If your exercises do not feel good, or if you experience internal resistance while doing them, then you should adjust your intention by focusing upon smaller prizes at first. Get some wins under your belt, feel good about winning, be thankful for what comes your way, and then expand your goals. A lady in Maryland who won over a million dollars in the lottery was quoted as saying that she treated all her wins like they were big jackpots. She was excited, thankful, and she always expected to win a grand prize, which she got. She went on to say that she never expressed negative feelings regarding money. She maintained her positivity and her vision for prosperity and abundance, and it showed up in the most amazing way…as a big lottery prize!

QUESTION: Can I force the Law of Attraction to work for me?

ANSWER: The Universal Law will not respond if you try to force it to work for you. *Forcing and demanding are strong affirmations that you don't believe that this creative power will work for you.* The nature of the Universal Law is to respond through the easiest, most effortless avenue of expression based upon what you are passionate about. If you are passionate about networking with people and making sales in this manner, then this power can and will help you become a more successful professional. If you are passionate about manifesting money through the Law of Attraction, then this power will respond to your intentions with mathematical certainty *as long as you persist in the feeling of the wish fulfilled,* that is, as long as you persist in feeling and imagining the reality of what you desire. This power meets you where you are and always responds to what you are emitting in terms of beliefs and feelings. Energy goes where your attention goes, but you cannot force this power to respond because its nature does not respond to forcing or coercing. It will give you what you desire as long as:

- You have expressed a clear intention
- You can fully accept and believe in the reality of what you desire
- You persist in feeling the reality of what you desire

QUESTION: How long will it take for me to get results?

ANSWER: If you had complete faith that your intention could manifest today, then your desire would manifest today, but most people do not have the faith required to make an instantaneous manifestation. As a result, we must resort to using the various tools of consciousness to help us expand our beliefs. As we monitor our words and as we use the power of creative visualization to expand our beliefs and expectations, we gradually move into a state of consciousness that allows us to manifest what we desire. *You will have what you desire when your belief is equal to your desire.*

QUESTION: What if I have difficulty imagining myself winning a big lottery prize?

ANSWER: The fact that you cannot imagine winning a large lottery prize could mean that you are not yet ready for a big win or that there is some internal resistance that prevents you from attracting a lot of money. The key here is to start small and then expand slowly and continuously. Begin imagining yourself winning smaller prizes, feel the reality of smaller wins, and then expand your creative visualization exercises to reflect larger wins as you become more comfortable with having more money. As you visualize your desires daily, you gradually become more comfortable with what you want to manifest. This is the key to effective creative visualization. Do not rush through this process if this is where you find yourself. Do the exercises regularly until you feel better about receiving more money, and then go for the gold.

QUESTION: Do you really believe that anyone can use the Law of Attraction to win the lottery?

ANSWER: I believe that the Law of Attraction can be used by any person who is willing to learn about this creative power and persist with a clearly defined action plan until the manifestation has taken place. You don't have to be particularly smart or a child of royalty to use this power effectively. The Universal Law does not have an opinion about how much money you should have, so you might as well make up your mind to get what you want. *I have learned that those people who manifest what they desire from the Law of Attraction usually persist just a bit longer than those who give up.* The Universal Law loves persistence, so keep this in mind as you work on manifesting the desires of your heart. A very good friend from Los Angeles was a contestant on the TV game show called THE PRICE IS RIGHT where she won thousands of dollars in cash during her appearance. She is a student of the Law of Attraction who has also won lots of contest prizes and casino jackpots, including one for nearly $40,000.00. She attributes her good fortune to a positive attitude, affirmations and to the regular use of creative visualization. Her morning ritual includes fifteen to twenty minutes of creative visualization in which she imagines living a rich and prosperous lifestyle. Weeks before flying to Las Vegas she begins her ritual of visualizing herself winning slot machine jackpots, and in her imagination she hears the electronic buzz of the machines as she wins money. She wins money more often than not, and she always practices gratitude for every win. When I asked what her winning secret is, she replied: "I always stick to a budget and I maintain a good attitude. I speak positive words and I use creative visualization each day to feel rich. *Feeling rich is the secret.*" As I began writing this book, a friend who is a certified Law of Attraction Coach from Los Angeles introduced me to a woman who won $250,000.00 on a California Lottery scratch off ticket. Prior to winning the top prize, this particular woman often visualized herself as a lottery winner. She said that no matter how much money she won, she always acted as though it was a big prize and acted accordingly in her feelings. Although I did not interview her for my book, she was kind enough to explain that she was always very positive with all her words, thoughts and feelings. She felt like a big winner even before she won her lottery prize. In a nutshell, the key to winning the lottery with the Law of Attraction is to express positive and expectant feelings on a continual basis. This method has worked for the author of this book, for everyone interviewed in this book, and it will work for the reader because the Law of Attraction can be used by everyone to the same degree. The factor that limits our manifestation is belief, which can be changed through creative visualization.

QUESTION: What other tips can you suggest to help manifest lottery prizes through the Law of Attraction?

ANSWER: The creative power within you responds to all your prolonged thoughts, feelings, and words, so you must be very aware of your mental state at all times. Do your best to make sure that all your thoughts, feelings and words are positive or neutral, at best. Every thought you think and feeling you express contributes to your overall mental atmosphere, so be aware of this fact at all times because your dominant thoughts and feelings will outpicture themselves in the physical world. Although it's not always easy to meet the challenges of life with a positive outlook, we should strive to be aware that we are creating events and circumstances that reflect our habitual thoughts.

QUESTION: What part does luck play in manifesting lottery prizes?

ANSWER: I do not believe in luck. I believe in randomness and intentional creation. In any lottery there must eventually be a winner considering the number of tickets sold and the odds of the game. For example, the odds of winning the Powerball are 1 in 175 million tickets. The odds of winning the New York State Pick 5 game are 1 in 575,000 tickets. This is where randomness comes into play since there will eventually be a winner if enough tickets are sold. The other side of the coin is that people can create their own fortune or "luck" through the use of intention. Some of the winners I have met have told me that they "knew" they would win one day. They used the power of intention and expectancy to manifest a lottery prize. *As we use the tools of manifestation daily and as we begin to see positive results, our expectation that more good is on the way will increase.* It is this expectation that will manifest the desires of your heart. In 2013, FOX News in Arizona reported the story about a couple from Tempe who won the lottery twice for $2,500,000.00 and then for $1,000,000.00. During a television interview, the winners revealed that they *expected* to win again and they attributed their good fortune to a positive attitude. The winning couple was so expectant about winning the lottery that they were quoted as saying that their win was not a matter of *if they would win, but when* they would win. In fact, the winning couple was later quoted by ABC NEWS as saying that beating the "odds had little to do with gambling, but more with self-belief." This story amply demonstrates that there is a tremendously creative power in expectancy and intention.

QUESTION: Someone once told me that I should ask for what I want once or visualize once and then release my intention. Is this true?

ANSWER: This is not true. A weight lifter does not lift weights once and a swimmer does not only swim once. In order to manifest your desires, you must persist in imagining what you desire until it manifests. Your job as a co-creator with the Universe is to persist in feeling the reality of your wish fulfilled until your manifestation has taken place. As you persist with these creative visualization exercises you will gradually become more comfortable with what you desire and you will be better able to manifest what you want. *The most creative force you have is feeling. What you feel, you create.* As you imagine daily, you feel better about having what you desire and it begins to show up in your life through expected and unexpected channels. The feeling power that I am referring to is not an excited pep-rally feeling, but a confident inner confidence confirming that what you desire is on the way.

QUESTION: Which particular exercise should I perform on a regular basis?

ANSWER: You should try each manifestation technique and determine which one feels best for you. The best advice I can offer is to commit to the exercise that feels best for you and that makes you feel good a majority of the time. Keep in mind that your feelings are creative, and these positive feelings are the catalyst that will bring you the financial abundance and the lottery prize you desire. Also keep in mind that you can and should create your own manifestation exercises based upon the mental scenes that feel good to you. Some people enjoy using the same exercise over and over while others use two or three exercises that feel good.

QUESTION: Should I perform these exercises in the same place and time each day?

ANSWER: Where and when you do these exercises is up to you. Some people enjoy doing their creative visualization exercises first thing in the morning while others do them throughout the day or in the evening. The important idea is to do them each day while focusing on feelings of wealth and abundance while doing them. A quiet place in which to visualize is preferred, but some people visualize while commuting to work with coworkers or while on the bus. Some people visualize during a break at work or during a relaxing bubble bath. A female friend who became very successful in the real estate business took time to visualize each morning before her spouse and children woke up. Unfortunately, some people wait for the perfect opportunity to visualize, but the truth is that there is no perfect time to visualize. A person who is serious about manifesting money through the law of Attraction should not wait until the stars are in alignment or until she is inspired to visualize. The perfect time is always now. In addition, do not become frustrated if your creative visualization exercises are challenging at first. Everyone experiences this at some time or other. At first, you may experience an inability to focus on your desires, your mind may wander during these exercises, or you might encounter challenges while trying to create an image of your desire during initial attempts. This is totally normal. The important thing is to persist because these exercises will become easier through daily commitment.

QUESTION: Should I tell my friends and family members that I am doing these exercises?

ANSWER: Absolutely not. The root word of secret is sacred, and the spiritual work that you are doing is made sacred by keeping it a secret. You will quickly dissipate your spiritual energy by telling people what you are doing. Your best plan of action is to keep all inner mental and spiritual work a secret by focusing on it daily, committing to these manifestation exercises, and by expanding your belief and expectation through this commitment. A person who is new to manifesting money through the Law of Attraction might not be firmly established in his faith to counteract the negative opinions of skeptical onlookers, so secrecy is the keynote as you begin these manifestation exercises. The author of this book kept his manifestation exercises a secret as he visualized his desires each day and worked on manifesting money through the Law of Attraction. You might want to share your interests with an online Law of Attraction community or you may have a friend or two who is on the same spiritual path that you are on, but the best plan of action is to keep your manifesting work a complete secret. Once you have manifested the money and the life you desire, then you can tell your friends and family members how you did it.

QUESTION: Can you guarantee that I will win the lottery using these manifestation techniques?

ANSWER: I cannot guarantee that you will win a lottery jackpot using these methods as much as a sporting goods salesman cannot guarantee that he will make you fit by selling you a treadmill. You must do the mental and spiritual work that is necessary to manifest your desires. I can guarantee that I have exposed you to the most effective methods of manifestation. Success through the Law of Attraction is attained through a change in consciousness and by creating an intention and then nurturing that intention through your thoughts, feelings, beliefs and actions. The person who is intent on manifesting financial abundance through the Law of Attraction can achieve his/her desires because the Universal Law is an impartial power that will work for anyone who commits to using it effectively. You can have all the money and opportunities that you desire if you learn to harness the power of your thoughts and feelings effectively. Throughout the years many people have learned to use the Law of Attraction successfully. Online forums, books and various CDs contain numerous testimonies of people who have won lottery prizes, contests, and manifested lots of money through this creative power. There is no limit to the abundance and prosperity that you can attain through the Law of Attraction. The question is, are you willing to do the spiritual work that is necessary to manifest your desires?

QUESTION: What is the six months rule as it applies to manifesting money?

ANSWER: I feel that it usually takes about six months of committed spiritual work to solidify an intention to the point where manifestation is inevitable. In addition, throughout the years I have taught a number of Law of Attraction classes after which various students have shared that some of their major intentions have taken at least six months of commitment to manifest. I am not saying that every manifestation will require six months of committed spiritual work nor am I suggesting that six months is the magic number. I am suggesting that a person who wants to manifest a lot of money be committed and patient enough to know that the seed of intention must be planted and then continually watered with faith and expectation in order for it to sprout. We live in a Universe that is governed by order and harmony. The order within the manifestation equation is demonstrated by the fact that the seed of intention must first be planted and then watered and exposed to the sunlight of faith and expectation. The harmony within the manifestation equation is disturbed when we express positivity one minute and then resort to negativity and inharmonious thoughts the next moment. In order to manifest our desires through the Law of Attraction we must approach this power in a balanced and harmonious manner until the manifestation has taken place. Although this is challenging at first, it becomes increasingly easy as time passes and as we realize just how creative our thoughts, feelings and words are.

QUESTION: Are there any other methods of winning the lottery through the Law of Attraction?

ANSWER: The only way to manifest money or to win the lottery through the Law of Attraction is through a change in consciousness. Good luck charms, talismans, incense, prayer cloths and incantations have no true power for the person who understands that true spiritual power is attained by aligning to the God force within. Christ, Buddha, and a host of other spiritual masters have taught us that the Kingdom of Heaven is within. Therefore, in order to manifest the life of your dreams you must go within your consciousness and create the spiritual blueprint of your desires in order to manifest them. "As within, so without" is not only a catchy phrase but a profound spiritual truth.

QUESTION: How should I act when I win money and manifest abundance through the Law of Attraction?

ANSWER: The way you act after you manifest money through the Law of Attraction is very important. *Do not act as if your manifestation is a miracle because there are no miracles within the Universal Law.* No matter how large your financial manifestation, you should not act as though you are experiencing a "lucky break" or that your manifestation is a special blessing. The money that comes your way is a reflection of your changing consciousness and your ability to align to the divine nature of the Universal Law. A few years ago after I had spent time visualizing myself winning lots of money, I drove to a casino in Palm Springs, California. Upon entering the casino I found a $100 bill on the pavement. I took this fortunate find as a sign that the Universal Law was reflecting back to me what I had put out in terms of faith and expectation. I used that particular $100 to play the slots, and ended up winning so much money that I left the casino a few hours later with over $3,000.00 stuffed in my pockets. At the end of the day I was very thankful for the money that I manifested at the casino, but I made a point not to consider what happened as a lucky break. If we consider a large financial manifestation a miraculous event, then we place these events into the realm of rare occurrences. Therefore, all your manifestations should be regarded as regularly occurring events.

QUESTION: Why are feelings so important when manifesting money through the Law of Attraction?

ANSWER: The Law of Attraction speaks the language of feelings, and it will respond to your prolonged feelings of prosperity and abundance with mathematical certainty. This is why it is very important to persist in feeling the reality of your wish fulfilled before the Universal Law can deliver your desires. Every Law of Attraction lottery winner and contest winner I have met has mentioned the importance of emotionally experiencing the reality of their fulfilled desire as a prerequisite to manifestation. Your prolonged feelings of financial abundance will attract the manifestation you desire because the nature of the Universal Law is to respond to what you are feeling on a consistent basis. If you feel rich and abundant more often, then you will experience circumstances that match your predominant feelings of abundance. If, however, you feel anxious, worried, and apprehensive about how you will meet your needs until your next paycheck, you will experience circumstances that match your predominant feelings of fear and anxiety. This is why the rich get richer and the poor get poorer; it's all a matter of feelings. You might want to become more aware of what you are feeling throughout the day by asking yourself: How do I feel about money? Do I feel that I deserve more money and abundance? Be honest about your answers, and if fear or doubt surfaces, embrace those feelings, and then work on releasing them through the use of spoken affirmations, creative visualization exercises, gratitude, and through the practice of receiving. *Your destiny is in your feelings, and you can always change what you are feeling.* This is why affirmations and creative visualization exercises are so powerful. When done on a consistent basis, they assist us in re-arranging our thoughts by creating positive beliefs and feelings that will enhance our lives in the long run.

QUESTION: Can these manifestation techniques be used to manifest other things, like cars, houses and jobs?

ANSWER: You can use these manifestation exercises to get anything that you can make a part of your beliefs and feelings. If you want a car or more money, then begin imagining having more money or the car of your dreams. Using your imagination, you should experience the feelings and sensations that you would experience if your dream were a reality. If you want a new girlfriend, for example, you should imagine being with that person and feeling the joy that you would experience while being in a fulfilling relationship. If you had a girlfriend, what would you say to her? Where would you go? How would she make you feel physically and emotionally? If you had a boyfriend, how would he treat you? How would you spend your time with him? Determine what you want, and then use your imagination to feel the reality of what you desire, and your desire will manifest through the most effortless avenue of expression. If you want a new car, for example, imagine owning that car. How would you feel to drive it? What would your friends say about your new car? How would the wind feel blowing through the windows as you drive this car? Feel the reality of owning the car, maintain this feeling, and the way will be made for you to have your dream car. *Do not focus on HOW you will get it, but focus on WHAT you want, and persist in feeling the reality of having it now.* Finally, do not wait for the perfect time to imagine your desires into reality. You do not have to light incense, use special chants, or dress in robes to visualize your desires into reality. Find a comfortable place to sit and relax, and then close your eyes and use your imagination and feelings to explore the reality of your fulfilled desire. Persist in imagining your desired reality, and the Universal Law will reward your commitment because the Universe loves persistence. Begin by visualizing for five minutes per day and then increase the time as you become more comfortable with these manifestation exercises. Eventually, you should be able to visualize for twenty minutes per day with enthusiasm and presence of mind. By that time, the events that unfold in your life will testify to the fact that your thoughts and feelings are highly creative.

QUESTION: What are some of the best manifestation books available?

ANSWER: The person who is serious about manifesting desires through the Law of Attraction should read the following books by Neville Goddard: THE LAW AND THE PROMISE, FEELING IS THE SECRET and THE POWER OF AWARENESS. Neville Goddard was a very insightful spiritual teacher whose basic message centered on the supremacy of human imagination and its ability to influence and create reality. His books have been read by millions of people throughout the world, and have helped just as many people achieve their dreams through the controlled use of imagination. Because Neville allowed people to record his various lectures, many of his speeches and recordings are available on YouTube. Another wonderful book about manifestation is MIRACLES by Stuart Wilde. Although a small book, it contains some of the most profound information about the Universal Law ever written, and it explains how to use the Law of Attraction effectively. Another helpful book about manifestation is WISHES FULFILLED: MASTERING THE ART OF MANIFESTING by Dr. Wayne Dyer. Relying heavily on the teachings of Neville Goddard, this book delves into the art and practice of manifestation in a way that is enlightening and easy to understand. The common denominator that runs through the books I have recommended and the manifestation techniques in this book is the dynamic power of feelings. *Your destiny is in your feelings,* and the more effectively you are able to harness the power of your feelings, the faster will you manifest your desires through the creative power of your intention.

Sensation precedes manifestation and is the foundation upon which all manifestation rests. Be careful of your moods and feelings, for there is an unbroken connection between your feelings and your visible world.

—Neville Goddard

PART 4: TIPS, SUGGESTIONS AND COMMON DENOMINATORS:

Y ou can manifest the life of your dreams through the Law of Attraction, but you must commit to this creative power and then learn to use it constructively on a daily basis for best results. The amount of spiritual work required differs with each person. Some people will manifest wonderful results after a few weeks of commitment while other people will take a bit longer to start seeing positive results. The best suggestion is to practice these exercises daily for best results. Faith without works is dead, and one cannot expect to manifest money by merely sitting on the couch and wishing for it. The creative power of the Universal Law is set in motion through the direction of your intention and through your daily actions. As you use the power of your spoken word to affirm abundance, your focus and intention switch from neutral to drive, and you will begin aligning yourself with places and situations that will help you manifest your desires. *Your job as a co-creator with the Universal Law is to use your words, feelings and imagination to bring your desires into manifestation. Don't worry about how and when your desire will manifest.*

The infinitely creative power of the Universal Law will work out the details. The Law of Attraction is guaranteed to work if you work it. When you get into the flow of using this power correctly, you will begin to see positive results that will encourage you to persist.

In addition, I want to add that half-hearted commitment will result in a half-hearted response from the Universal Law. We cannot expect to manifest our desires if we only commit to this power for five minutes per day. The path of manifestation requires that we embody the Universal Law in order for it to work for us. This means that all our thoughts, actions and feelings must be in alignment with our desires. It also means that we take the necessary actions to generate the belief that is required to translate our desires from the realm of spirit to the realm of expression.

THE COMMON DENOMINATORS AMONG LAW OF ATTRACTION LOTTERY WINNERS:

- All Law of Attraction lottery winners imagined the reality of being a winner through the persistent use of creative visualization. All winners were focused on what they would feel and experience as a winner, not on how their lottery win would take place. They focused on the end result at all times.

- All winners used their words creatively and positively all the time, never joking about money and never saying negative things about money. All their spoken words reflected the desired reality of being rich and prosperous.

- All winners persisted with these manifestation techniques on a daily basis through the use of the spoken word, creative visualization exercises, and feeling the reality of a lottery win.

- All winners kept their manifesting work a secret knowing that informing other people might encourage negative comments and other distracting elements.

- All winners adhered to a strict budget and gave thanks for each and every win along the way.

As I prepared the final section of this book I remembered a particular article about Cynthia Stafford, the famous Law of Attraction lottery winner who won a Mega Millions jackpot of $112,000,000.00 in May 2007. It was reported that for approximately four months she constantly imagined how she would feel to be rich and how she would feel to live an affluent lifestyle. During a television interview the lottery winner said, "The way to win is to visualize." During the same broadcast she also revealed, "I kept seeing myself holding that check and knowing that it was going to happen, and it did." Although she was a busy, single mother at the time, she made the effort to learn about the Law of Attraction, and then she put that knowledge into action through the use of creative visualization. Her manifestation action plan included learning about the Law of Attraction and doing the necessary mental and emotional work that was required to translate her desires from the invisible world of thoughts to the visible world of manifestation. Her big lottery jackpot and the jackpots of those individuals who were interviewed for this book are not rare examples of luck, but are clear examples that the creative power of intention can be used by any person who is willing to commit to a manifestation action plan until the end result is accomplished. Manifesting a lot of money with the Law of Attraction is not a miraculous event or a privilege set aside for certain people. It is the result of the correct use of spiritual law that is certain and unfailing. There are no miracles within the Universal Law.

Another famous winner whose manifestation method is worth mentioning is that of Helene Hadsell, whom I briefly mentioned during the introduction of this book. She is the subject of numerous articles, radio interviews and television shows, and is probably the most famous contest winner in the world. By the 1980s she had already won over 5,000 contest prizes, including five overseas trips to Europe for her entire family, and a new luxury home from the Formica Corporation. The winning entry for the new home was chosen from over two million entries! Her personal manifestation technique, also known as the "SPEC Technique", is very similar to that of the lottery winners I interviewed. Helene Hadsell's SPEC technique is as follows:

- **SELECT** A GOAL

- **PROJECT** IT (*feel the reality of having it now through creative visualization*)

- **EXPECT** IT

- **COLLECT** IT

Mrs. Hadsell, who in 1958 was influenced by the famous book titled THE POWER OF POSITIVE THINKING by Norman Vincent Peale, was quoted as saying that her SPEC technique was not new or unique. Like Mrs. Hadsell, the lottery winners whom I interviewed followed a similar technique in which they selected their goal, and then projected it through their feelings until they expected it, and finally they collected their winnings. I can corroborate that this technique works because my manifestation technique is the same as that of the other lottery winners.

I would like to encourage readers to persist in the "feeling of the wish fulfilled" because in this persistent feeling you will manifest your desires. By far, the most important lesson that I have learned about manifestation is the importance of feelings. It is the language of the Universal Law and the currency that you will use to pay for your manifestation. Your desire to manifest more money through the Law of Attraction is not a selfish desire, but an evolutionary impulse to evolve and experience more abundance as part of your birthright. The nature of your soul is to expand and evolve in every way possible, and once you begin this journey all the spiritual encouragement, power and inspiration will come to you because abundance is your natural state of being. The first step is always the most challenging, but as you learn more about the art of manifestation and as you persist in projecting your desires into the Universal Law, the manifestations that appear along the way will encourage you to persist and to create more abundance for yourself.

During March 2014 the Huffington Post, Time Magazine and USA Today reported the story about a couple from Virginia who won the lottery three times in one single month. During the month of March 2014 this couple won $1,000,000.00 on the Powerball, then another $50,000.00 on the Virginia Pick Four, and finally they won $1,000,000.00 from a scratch off ticket. A few months later, national news sources reported that a man from Indianapolis won two separate $1,000,000.00 prizes within three months in Indiana's Hoosier Lottery. These stories demonstrate the fact that lottery players are winning big prizes all the time, and some people win more than once. Some of these players spend years wishing for that "one lucky break" while others commit to manifesting their desires through the Law of Attraction. This dynamic, spiritual power has helped millions of people around the world manifest the life of their dreams, and so can you! There is so much money out there with your name on it that you owe it to yourself to use the power of intention to manifest the life of your dreams. Begin now to expand your personal vision to include unlimited prosperity, and you will soon discover that the events and circumstances of your life will irresistibly take the form of your thoughts, words, and feelings of abundance. The Universe is waiting for you to step forward and claim your jackpot.

If you would like to learn more about the Law of Attraction, please check out my other books:

ADVANCED LAW OF ATTRACTION TECHNIQUES: MASTERING MANIFESTATION AND ATTRACTING WHAT YOU WANT FAST

MANIFEST YOUR MILLIONS: A LOTTERY WINNER SHARES HIS LAW OF ATTRACTION SECRETS

Printed in Poland
by Amazon Fulfillment
Poland Sp. z o.o., Wrocław
04 August 2022

814782f0-bf71-4870-96bd-07636f83478eR01